SHAPING ME

SHAPING ME

Amanda Saltarelli

Copyright © 2020 by Amanda Saltarelli.

ISBN:	Softcover	978-1-9845-8453-3
	eBook	978-1-9845-8452-6

All rights reserved. No part of this book may be reproduced or transmitted in any form or by any means, electronic or mechanical, including photocopying, recording, or by any information storage and retrieval system, without permission in writing from the copyright owner.

Any people depicted in stock imagery provided by Getty Images are models, and such images are being used for illustrative purposes only. Certain stock imagery © Getty Images.

Illustrations by Savannah Stuckey

Print information available on the last page.

Rev. date: 06/22/2020

To order additional copies of this book, contact:
Xlibris
1-888-795-4274
www.Xlibris.com
Orders@Xlibris.com
815319

For the most amazing people,
 & simply calling out the rest

To the people who betrayed me:

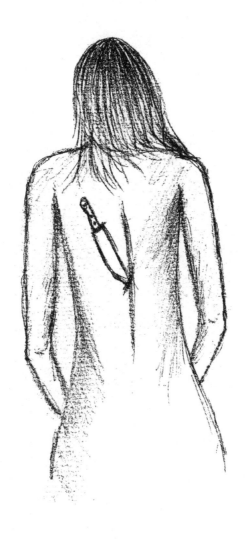

I'd wait for your call, sitting by the phone.
Allowing the anxiety to possess my soul,
hoping your heart would slowly unfold.
I knew you were emotionally unavailable.
But I fell too quickly and my heart was too breakable.
-*Can't be with or without you*

Isn't it strange?
Knowing we deserve better.
Knowing we could get better.
But yet, we stay because there's some twisted excitement in being with someone
who treats us like an option.
Every day we feed off of wondering; will they choose me?
-A messed up thing regarding the human mind

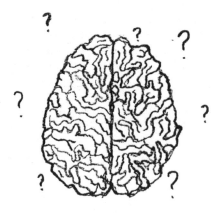

"You're crazy"
-*Every guys go to insults*

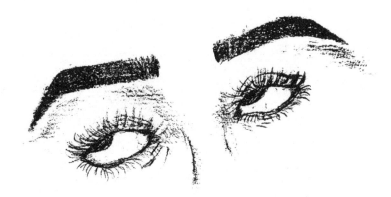

I am going to have to pass.
Pass on your half ass love.
Pass on your half ass attention.
-Swiping left

You always told me that I expected too much.
The only thing I ever wanted from
you, was a sign that you cared.
And the fact that I needed a sign, was
a sign that you did not care.
-*screw you*

"I'm not ready for a relationship."
   -bullshit

To the "friend" that I defended when
the whole school slut-shamed you.
I do not appreciate you stabbing me in the back,
and befriending the girl who said even worse things
about me than the boys who talked about you.
-*You are why I keep my circle small*

This is to the "friend" who went
out with my first love
two days after I vented to you
about all the damage he caused
my heart, and self-esteem.
-You are also the reason I keep my circle small

I used to like the boys
I knew I shouldn't.
I always forgave the ones
who didn't deserve my forgiveness. And we all do it
because we all want love. Sometimes we don't care
where it comes from. It's just something we need.
 -*Sometimes we drink water from the sink*

And there I was,
loving up on a guy who was waiting for another girl
to text him back.
Meanwhile,
I waited for him to pay attention to me
-*What am I doing?*

I was falling for someone whose attention was on everything and every **girl,**
but me.
-This night really sucks

I found out an old flame ended things
because I was too clingy.
He had never been more right,
because when I see a gorgeous face,
I cling on to it, hoping it will make me gorgeous too.
-I got too excited and clung onto the idea of us

I have a tendency to hold onto things
that have been gone for far too long.
-I'm either sentimental or stupid

I need to learn to refrain from
telling boys my feelings because
once I do the chase is up,
and I see them running in the other direction.
-*I hate playing games*

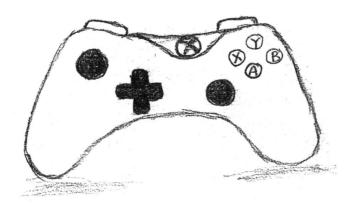

Here I sit, all ready,
all done up,
because I rely on unreliable people.
-This is more than just a rain check, it's a reflection
of how much you care

Gemini, why'd you get so scared?
Was my ability to love too much to handle?
*-Everyone avoids feelings, other
people's, and their own*

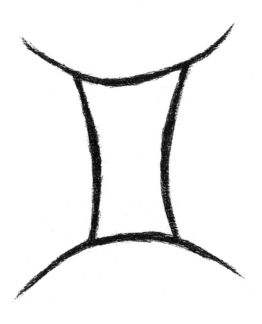

I try and plant seeds in
the boys who will never love me.
-I am running out

I hope you die,
but sometimes I wish I would too
-So I guess it doesn't mean that much

My heart found its way to your lap. It jumped out at you, and maybe it scared you. Maybe I don't know what scares you, and maybe what I did was your fear. Let me tell you what monsters lay beneath my bed. What gives me paralyzing fear? Giving your heart to someone, and they decide they don't want it.
 -*Two different streets*

You walked into my life,
and this shift took place in my life,
in my mentality,
and my heart.
It was all making room for you.
Then you walked out,
and now there is just emptiness
where you are supposed to be
-Those green eyes made me blind to reality.

My brown eyes were no match for your green.
I was hypnotized, and my nieve heart did not want
to believe that I wasn't in yours.
You weren't really in my heart, just my shirt.
-*My mistake*

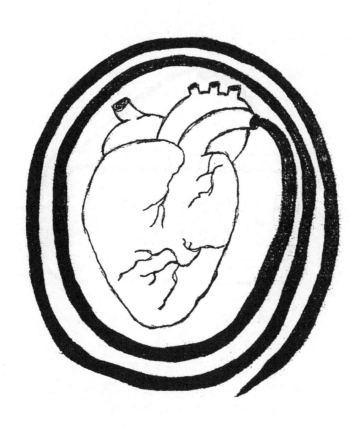

I always begged for your attention. Begged
for you to tell me how you felt.
Even though I needed your words to
survive, you just kept them to yourself.
-*Never beg for someone's love*

I don't have many friends.
Which is most likely a result of
my values that many girls lack
-*loyalty*

To a boy who I claimed to love when I was young.
I never loved you.
I never knew what love looked like and
you tried to convince me you were the
only one who could ever show me.
I was young and foolish, and I believed
your overprotectiveness came from a
place of love. I have grown up and
realized it came from a place of insecurity.
-Don't confuse abuse for love

My father who was supposed to be there as a guide, acted more like a scared boy.
All he knows how to do is run and hide.
- Maybe that's why I find myself attracted to those who fear commitment.

I thought the second boy I fell in love with was an angel.
I'd write poems about his eyes and the safety I felt in his arms.
But in the end like everyone else, his true colors were exposed.
His pretty eyes liked to wander,
And suddenly he became content with our relationship being something he could dishonor.
-I hope she was worth it

My father was the man who hurt me the most.
A man who never let anyone get too close.
A man who was there, but only as a ghost. Could see him when he let you,
And disappears when you ask too many questions.
A man who ran away from anything that caused pain.
If you disagree with him, suddenly you are insane.
The man who I am half of,
the man who is supposed to give me the most love.
The man who leaves when push comes to shove.
-I am done waiting for you to step up to the plate

To love someone for almost two years,
and have them betray you will result in tears.
To find out the person that you begged not to lie to you fed you everything but the truth.
Your world comes crashing down and you realize everything is temporary in youth.
Despite the love that you felt, the loyalty you delt,
It wasn't enough for them to not want to hurt you.
Because when you truly don't want to hurt someone, you don't.
When it comes to loving someone right, I know he won't.
-*Just a heartless man is what I diagnose.*

Because you cheated,
I hope you worry about the next.
Due to your own infidelity,
I hope your brain becomes possessed.
I hope you imagine her doing the things you did to me, that is my only request.
The anxiety,
The bad feeling in your chest.
The idea of her body on someone else's,
That is a hard picture to digest.
The only thing I ever wanted was just a little ounce of respect.
You and I don't think the same, there's a bit of a disconnect. You aren't my problem,
and I am glad we never progressed.
Here's to me moving on,
I promise you will be impressed.
-My second love who turned out to be worse than the first

To the boys that made love seem like a good idea and then proved why it wasn't:

The one who made love exist for me,
and the one that ruined it.
-My first love

I gave you the roses from my heart,
you gave me thorns from yours.
-That was not a fair trade.

Meeting you, was hope.
Loving you, was a new discovery.
You gave me life
but managed to **almost** be the death of me.
-I hate you

I was overprotective because
I didn't want to lose you. In the end,
I lost you because
I was overprotective.
-Was I suffocating you?

When I first saw you
I was lost for words,
and now I have too many.
-You took my tongue and then spit it back at me

*"Who is that?"
-My curiosity and desire for a pretty face has
always been one of my greatest motivations.
The love that I never saw at home
was the love I was in search of.
I started my journey to find love
with a face that looked like trouble.
Spoiler alert: we found love,
but we were too young
and dumb to keep it.*

After we broke up,
I went on a date
and ended up spending
forty-five minutes talking about you.
-*Poor guy*

Falling in love is
the best thing,
until the one you love falls out of it.
-And that is hell

You were disguised as an angel.
Falling to my rescue,
lifting me up,
glorifying me to my face, but
stabbing me in the back.
I claimed you were an angel,
but I guess I was blind to the horns poking out of your head.
-*Devil*

But what do you do
when the boy of your dreams
becomes a reality only to
become a nightmare.
-*I wish I could wake up*

Crying your heart out. Begging God to either
bring them back, or get over them.
Begging for signs that never come. Hearing
their name and instant anxiety.
Sleeping in your bed missing
when they once did too.
Hearing that they are dating someone
else, and trying not to let the jealousy take
over your mind. Staring at your phone,
waiting for a call that never comes.
Not being able to move on because you
still imagine yourself with only them.
-*Heartbreak*

It is one of the hardest things to do
-Ignore your calls

I either love you, or myself.
But It's impossible to have both.
I used to always choose you.
-Now I am choosing me

I don't know what is harder to believe,
that you hurt me so many times,
or that I kept letting you.
-Self worth is so important

There was always a bitter truth
beneath your sweet lips.
 -*You are such a liar*

Everyone thought they had us all figured out.
I was the crazy ex that was still
madly in love with you.
And as much as you tried to convince
everyone around you,
including yourself that you didn't want me anymore.
Your calls and obsessive attempts to talk
to me convinced me otherwise.
-Everyone thought it was so black and white.

I have no words. Just emotions.
Confusion, anger, sadness.
-You did not deserve me

Most of my dreams consist of you betraying me.
My heart cannot get over the fact that even
my second love, who was my best friend,
took a knife and placed it into my back.
The boy with the sweet smile, and "caring
heart", found so much pleasure in turning
the knife, and doing whatever it took
to have the power to hurt me.
-Get out of my head

How can two people be so
wrong for each other,
but it still feels so right.
- *Dangerous chemistry*

You were the love of my life,
and now you aren't even a part of it.
-The way life works

I have always been a strong believer that people
who have the same heart, end up together.
That is why I was so blindsided when
you abruptly broke my heart.
Because you had convinced me and
pretended that we had the same one.
-That wasn't fair

I don't understand your heart.
But I don't understand mine either
because after all the pain you put me through
I still have the ability to picture a life with you.
-*Stupidity*

It has almost been a year since the day you left.
Since the day i wept,
begging you to stay.
You told me you loved me.
-Clearly not enough

How is it we know each other so well but it feels like we don't know each other at all?
-Break ups are so weird

You always creep into my mind
while I'm asleep, unguarded.
Get out of my head, I feel haunted.
-*Dreams*

I used to think about you every minute,
then eventually it was every hour,
and now I think about you less
and less everyday.
Sadly, I still think about you everyday
but at least I know I'm healing.
-*I won't be broken forever*

I should have known that your good looks and kind heart were too good to be true. I should have known that your lips were poisoning my mind into believing your lies. I should have known that a boy so young is incapable of keeping an eternal promise. I should have known that love when you're sixteen is temporary. I should have known that you weren't honest. I should have known that you were hand making a knife before you placed it into my back. I should have known that our love, like everything else, had an expiration date. I should have known that eventually you would leave. I should have known that we would come to an end like everything else in my life. I should have known when you left the fourth time that you truly had no intentions of consistently staying in my life. I should have known that you didn't love me. I should have assumed that you didn't love me unconditionally. I should have known that you were going to break my heart.
   -But how could I have known?

All I can do is wait for time to take you away
and turn you into a distant memory.
-Someday you won't mean anything

My mind was too developed,
too strong,
too powerful for you.
-You could not handle it

I would have done anything for you.
But you hurt me so badly,
that you drove me away.
I had to leave.
I had to stop answering your calls.
I had to stop allowing you to suck me back in.
How is it you made me feel whole,
but so incomplete. So when I left.
-Just know, I did it for me

Were you surprised that I didn't welcome
you back into my life with open arms?
Are you shocked that I didn't jump
with excitement when you called
needing something from me?
I see right through you.
I see your hideous colors. I see your motivation that
only consists of benefiting you.
-Answering your calls with nothing but annoyance

Thank you for giving me something
to write about for so long,
but I am finally letting you go.
-*Goodbye to my first love*

I fell in love once,
and that ended in pain. I fell in love again,
and I went a little insane.
The two boys who I gave my heart to turned out to be almost the same.
That's why i'm guarded,
but a stronger person I became.
-That's the only good thing you did.

My second love made me feel crazy for having a doubt.
So Imagine how I felt when I found out.
My trust does not come easily due to people treating me evilly.
You proved me right,
I am amazed that you are able to sleep at night.
-You should have let me go

Long distance was as hard as can be.
Your hands were on her while I wished they were on me.
I paid the price of loving you when It should have been free.
I told you my fears and you heard my cries, I always had an appetite for the truth,
all you ever fed me were lies.
I am moving on, and you will jump to the next. Karma will come, you better watch your step.
-*Trust issues*

To the people who saved me:

My best friend,
Is the most amazing person I have ever met
How rare to find a person with all the same values,
and the same heart
-soulmates

"Do not give your pearls to pigs" - My mom
-I should have listened

My five year old sister makes me want to protect
all the little girls and boys in this world.
-She asked me to write about her

And everytime you leave,
I whisper "I love you" as you walk away.
If you accidentally heard me,
what would you say?
-I love you, and I never thought I would be able to say that again

I know you say **love** is overused,
and maybe you're right.
But there is something about your smile,
and the way I feel when I am in your
arms that makes me believe that
what we have is special and that what we have is
love. Maybe, love is just love, and you are just you,
and maybe I am just falling
completely in love with you.
*-I fell in love and you fell into the
bed of someone else's*

The moment you told me you loved me was like winning independence from heartbreak.
-If you love me, that's a win

Be with someone who makes you strive to be better.
Someone who helps you see the important things in life.
-Be with someone who lifts you up

You have molded and reshaped my heart that was once damaged. You have kissed me and revived me of the brokenness I let take over me. You resurrected the girl I forgot I was, the parts of myself that I lost. I have felt more like myself with you in these past few months, then I have in the past year. You have shown me what love should feel like, the mutual respect there should be. You have shown me that it is possible to not cross lines, it just depends on how much someone values you.
-Thank you for treating me right, and showing me the way love should be (written in September of 2018)
Rewrite May of 2020:
You have reshaped my heart that was once damaged and made it even more unrecognizable. You have kissed me, revived me of the brokenness, and then poisoned me with a stronger effect that I almost let take over me. You resurrected the girl I forgot I was and helped me dig deep to find the parts of myself I lost, and then you destroyed them. I have felt like a different person these last couple of months without you. You have shown me what love should not feel like, and that there should be mutual respect between two people. You have shown me that it is possible for someone to look you in the eye and swear they value you enough to not cross lines and then go ahead and do it anyway.
-Thank you for treating me wrong, and showing me the way love should never be

I didn't know I was gonna fall this hard. I didn't know that it was possible to feel so nervous but so comfortable around someone at the same time.
-It feels like I was made for you, and you were made for me

I have never felt a love so deep.
A love so strong it makes me weep.
A heart too perfect that I want to permanently keep.
-Crazy, and in love? Or crazy in love?

I can't get you out of my head.
And I don't know how to get back to mine.
-I am out of my mind

I will forever be thankful for the comfort and warmth you gave me when I needed you the most. I cannot thank you enough for being the glue that held me together when everything around me fell apart.

-No matter what happens, I am forever grateful for you. **(Unless you cheat on me, therefore this poem is now irrelevant.)**

There is going to be a time when you are no longer in my life. And I will truly understand why you were put in my life, but I don't know if I will ever understand why you had to be taken out.
- *You are too amazing to ever let go of (***Unless you cheat on me)**

And even long before it may end, I will still picture the day that you meet someone new. A new girl, a new town, and new love. I will see a post, I will see her. I will stalk her social media, I will drive myself insane, asking myself if you love her more than you loved me. I will wonder if she makes you laugh as hard as me. Does she cook for you? Does she constantly remind you how much you mean to her? Does she write you love letters? And I will not know the answer to any of these, except does she love you better than I did? And I will confidently be able to say no. Because the way I felt about you, and the way I loved you cannot be copied or beaten. My love is rare, and I am the type of person who will always care.
   -I am not saying I'm the best, but I promise I love better than the rest

Before I met you,
I didn't have a favorite color.
But suddenly I looked into your eyes
and I found my two greatest loves.
-You and blue

Making you laugh
-My greatest accomplishment

My best friend,
the boy I love all in one.
-Perfect, until you lose two in one

If we have the same heart, we will end up together.
-If not then it will end

My best friend has been the most stable person.
Even after all of the fake friends left,
and even after all the temporary boys exited my life.
She always remained, with a mop,
to clean up the mess that was made.
-I truly have the best friend

Family isn't always your blood.
Sometimes it is the people who love you the same way your family loves you.
Whoever you consider family,
those are the people you hold onto.
-Those are the people who will always be there

Limited people stay.
Limited people have truly shown they care.
In the end, I had to also save myself.
I had to change my mentality in order to survive.
I had to take my pain, and change the way I look at life.
And i had to separate my pain, and decide what to do with it.
- I am a survivor of my own mind,
my own mistakes, and my shitty taste in humans

I want to thank my best friend's parents for treating me more like their own then the people who were actually supposed to.
-*Literal angels*

I was so lucky to get such an amazing mom. She didn't have to be overbearing,
all she had to be was understanding. So when I become a good mom,
I know it will be thanks to her.
-For showing me what that looks like

My grandma is a prime example of starting from the bottom and rising to the top.
I admire her a lot.
She's faced her struggles and she's made her mistakes.
But a person is rewarded for the good decisions they make.
She's been there to help and guide me to where I should go.
I was blessed to have her in my life, that I know.
-thank you for supporting my dreams

My mother had to play both parts,
because having a good father wasn't in my cards.
She was always there to offer advice,
the only one there through all my stages of life.
I hope someday I can give her it all,
she's experienced too much strife.
But having her in my life is the most precious prize.
-I am blessed to have her

The women in my life are strong.
The impact they leave will be lifelong.
The women who never felt like they belong,
The women who the world treated so wrong.
They shaped who I am,
and they will shape who I become.
It's about where you go, not where you come from.
-*Amy, Ivy, Kristina, Maureen, Savannah*

I never had a male role model growing up.
Just men who never made me feel enough.
Men who were never true to their word,
But still managed to get angry when you'd call their bluff.
There is one man who gives me hope that all men aren't the same.
A man who doesn't try to make a woman go insane.
A man who can say sorry and not immediately try to blame.
A man who helped shape who my best friend became.
-My best friend's dad. The best man I've ever met.

To my readers, the things I learned:

We ignore the boys who fall for us,
and we fall for the boys who ignore us.
We settle for the ones who treat us like shit,
And then we complain about it.
-Irony

In between your legs is not the
way to your heart.
-Do not let the boys convince you otherwise.

The only pearls that pigs have
are the ones I gave them.
*-Stop giving pearls to the ones
who do not deserve them.*

If the beginnings are sweet,
it's going to be immensely sour when they leave.
-Be careful

Just like almost every wound, your
heartbreak will heal too.
You may still miss them,
but eventually the ache you once felt will stop.
-Hope

I am a romantic,
love is hopeless,
but we make a good team.
-Hopeless romantic

My heart,
so beautifully broken, still gives off love.
Hoping to receive it.
-What a sad disappointment

I have swallowed my tongue.
I have nodded in false agreement.
I have endured pain.
I have been something I'm not.
Just for a greater chance of love.
Even if that meant fake happiness.
-What a sad thing to settle for

Love,
I weep for you. I crave you.
I want you so bad.
-*save me*

I apologize to my heart.
I give you away constantly.
I let unworthy people break you.
From now on, it won't be as
easy. You keep breaking.
But things are changing.
I am changing.
I have reached a certain point.
-My breaking point

They try and get into your pants,
And we stupidly believe they will
next try to get into our hearts.
-Silly girl

The pretty faces suck me in.
Why do you think my love life
has been so messy?
-*Tornado*

You can have my heart.
-*Just proceed with caution*

I hate looking in the mirror sometimes.
It is too easy to point out things I dislike.
-very rarely do I find anything i like

But what do you do when the most dangerous place for you to be is in your own head?
-There is no escape

My heart wants love
But every love i've ever known
ends with me in tears,
and accomplished fears.
-Scared

Some days are better than others.
Some days I feel like I'm drowning.
Some days are a long battle,
and I have to fight off my own thoughts.
-*Depression*

Don't let them into your room because
even when they are long gone,
you will remember the feeling of them in your bed.
The laughs that echoed.
It's so unfair to let someone ruin your safe space.
-Letting them in your heart hurts enough

Dear love,
I used to imagine what you'd be
like, where i'd find you.
I used to picture being a teenager and
falling in love with a dreamy boy.
But what I never in depth thought about
was losing you.
I never prepared myself for how
heartbreaking that would be.
-I don't think anyone can

My heart is broken.
And I think a little part of it always will be.
My mind is strong,
and that's how I hold myself together.
-*Mentality is **everything***

Everyone does me wrong.
I am tired of singing the same song.
-My heart break playlist is always on

You have some say in who breaks your heart,
because you have to supply the power.
Sadly, I have a track record that consists
of giving my golden heart to the hands of thorns.
-*I break my own heart*

Heartbreak or love
-I always feel one or the other

The fires that are started by my family always burn bridges the fastest.
- sometimes slower for others

We play too many games when we are young
that keeps us from ever really becoming real.
And that's why everything seems so fake.
That's why everything feels so flimsy. Illusions
come crashing down, and so do all of our worlds.
-I want something real for once

It has become too casual to get into bed with someone that we don't even know.
-There seems to be a lack of love

The only result falling in love has,
is falling apart.
-Someone put me back together

I have a wild heart and a fiery temper.
-Do not test me

Sometimes people hold onto even the simplest of things that may give them happiness.
Because sometimes in life, nothing else makes them happy anymore
-sometimes no one understands

Out of all the days i've lived I feel the most alone, and the most unwanted today.
-I am literally drowning in my own tears

I think the saddest realization is
that if you were to tell someone to come to your
rescue right now,
no one would come,
because no one would care enough to.
-*so sad*

People say they love you,
but then they hurt you.
I say I love myself,
but then I hurt myself.
-This does not seem right

I don't think my ability to love so dramatically is a gift but instead a curse.
Because when the ones you love are unable to reciprocate the love you have given them.
It ruins you.
-It kills you a little inside

I love and hate myself
-Is that even possible

At least once,
we stared at the speeding cars.
And for just a second,
wondered what it would be like
to jump in front of them.
-who has?

Your heart will mend.
Your aches and your consuming loneliness will end.
And you may be drowning, but you are still breathing, despite the fact that you feel like you can't catch a breath.
Never let your temporary pain be your final emotion of life.
I promise there is more in the world than the pain that it gave you.
> *-Go find what the world made you forget you deserved*

1. You aren't going to marry them, young love lasting is rare, never assume that you are the exception.
2. If they really loved you, they would not leave or ever put themselves in a position to lose you.
3. Sometimes a person's version of always and forever is only eight months.
4. Your time is so precious, it is the only thing you cannot buy, earn, or ever get back
5. People can change. Be horrible, change, and then even go back to being horrible.
6. Sorry means nothing when they keep doing it over and over again
7. You can hate your body, but remind yourself how much it loves you. It heals you even when you are the one to cause it harm.
8. How to love
9. If you do not trust them, you should not be with them
10. If you have to choose between loving someone and loving yourself, please always choose yourself

-Ten things I learned in 2017

To all the girls who read this.
Stand with each other,
I know it's easier to stand against
each other than with.
But hating each other over nothing,
or simply out of jealousy
will just poison your own soul with hatred.
Support each other,
Support your friends even more.
Life is already too difficult for us,
we need to bring each other up,
rather than tear each other down.
-We are all going through the same things

There were some decisions that shouldn't have been made.
The wrong idea that people will always stay.
Choosing a path, and then realizing you went the wrong way.
In situations where you don't know what to say.
Every choice you make determines where you end up on your final day.
Always fight for yourself, but always know when to walk away.
Stay true to yourself, I promise you will find your way.
Where you find the people who end up in your life will usually determine if they are right.
Listen to your intuition, and be patient even when you have no hope left.
All you can do is fight for your happiness and always try your best.
-My advice

Made in the USA
Las Vegas, NV
26 November 2022